D1242494

AWESOME DOGS

Pugs

by Kari Schuetz

BLASTOFF! READERS
2

BELLWETHER MEDIA • MINNEAPOLIS, MN

This edition first published in 2017 by Bellwether Media, Inc.

No part of this publication may be reproduced in whole or in part without written permission of the publisher. For information regarding permission, write to Bellwether Media, Inc., Attention: Permissions Department, 5357 Penn Avenue South, Minneapolis, MN 55419.

Library of Congress Cataloging-in-Publication Data

Names: Schuetz, Kari, author.
Title: Pugs / by Kari Schuetz.
Description: Minneapolis, MN : Bellwether Media, Inc., 2017. | Series:
    Blastoff! Readers. Awesome Dogs | Includes bibliographical references and
    index. | Audience: Ages 5 to 8. | Audience: Grades K to 3.
Identifiers: LCCN 2016033339 (print) | LCCN 2016042999 (ebook) | ISBN
    9781626175587 (hardcover : alk. paper) | ISBN 9781681032795 (ebook)
Subjects: LCSH: Pug–Juvenile literature.
Classification: LCC SF429.P9 S38 2017 (print) | LCC SF429.P9 (ebook) | DDC
    636.76–dc23
LC record available at https://lccn.loc.gov/2016033339

Text copyright © 2017 by Bellwether Media, Inc. BLASTOFF! READERS and associated logos are trademarks and/or registered trademarks of Bellwether Media, Inc. SCHOLASTIC, CHILDREN'S PRESS, and associated logos are trademarks and/or registered trademarks of Scholastic Inc.

Editor: Betsy Rathburn   Designer: Lois Stanfield

Printed in the United States of America, North Mankato, MN.

Table of Contents

What Are Pugs?

Pugs are fun dogs with funny faces. Big eyes stick out above their flat **muzzles**.

4

Forehead wrinkles make the dogs look worried or confused.

Pugs are small but **stout**.
They weigh less than
20 pounds (9 kilograms).

The **breed** belongs to the **Toy Group** of the **American Kennel Club**.

Masked Dogs

All pugs are either black or **fawn** in color.

Their **coats** stay short. The hair is soft and smooth to touch.

thumbprint mark
↓

A pug's head is round. Some people think the shape looks like a fist.

Pug Profile

curled tail

black mask

flat face

face and neck wrinkles

Life Span: 13 to 15 years

Trainability:

1 2 3 4 5 6

Hardest to train   Easiest to train

A black mask covers the muzzle. A **thumbprint** mark stands out on the forehead.

The dog's ears are black
and folded. They look like
upside-down triangles.

The tail is curled. Some pug tails curl tightly enough to form two loops!

Pugs have been around for more than 2,000 years. Their history traces back to China.

China

N
W · E
S

Buddhist monks in Tibet
kept the dogs as pets.

Much later, **royals** in Europe made pugs part of their families.

Now American dog owners have loved the breed for more than 100 years!

Pugs are at their best when indoors. Hot, sticky weather is not safe for them.

18

The short-muzzled dogs can
easily **overheat**.

Inside their homes, pugs
follow their owners around
for food.

The dogs also look for chances to cuddle. Time to snore!

Glossary

American Kennel Club—an organization that keeps track of dog breeds in the United States

breed—a type of dog

Buddhist monks—religious men who give their whole lives to the teachings of Buddha

coats—the hair or fur covering some animals

fawn—a light brown color

muzzles—the noses and mouths of some animals

overheat—to become too hot

royals—kings, queens, and other members of ruling families

stout—solid and strong in build

thumbprint—the pattern of the thumb

Toy Group—a group of the smallest dog breeds; most dogs in the Toy Group were bred to be companions.

To Learn More

AT THE LIBRARY

Barnes, Nico. *Pugs*. Minneapolis, Minn.: ABDO Kids, 2015.

Beal, Abigail. *I Love My Pug*. New York, N.Y.: PowerKids Press, 2011.

Landau, Elaine. *Pugs Are the Best!* Minneapolis, Minn.: Lerner Publications Co., 2011.

ON THE WEB

Learning more about pugs is as easy as 1, 2, 3.

1. Go to www.factsurfer.com.

2. Enter "pugs" into the search box.

3. Click the "Surf" button and you will see a list of related web sites.

With factsurfer.com, finding more information is just a click away.

Index